THE BOY WHO OPENED THE HEAVENS

WRITTEN BY RON ISAACS
ILLUSTRATED BY BARBARA GERSON

Copyright ©2024 by Ron Isaacs (Higher Ground Books & Media). All rights reserved. No part of this publication may be reproduced in any form, stored in a retrieval system, or transmitted in any form, or by any means (electronic, mechanical, photocopying, recording or otherwise) without prior permission by the copyright owner and the publisher of this book

Higher Ground Books & Media
Springfield, OH
http://www.highergroundbooksandmedia.com

Printed in the United States of America 2024

Dedication:

For Leora

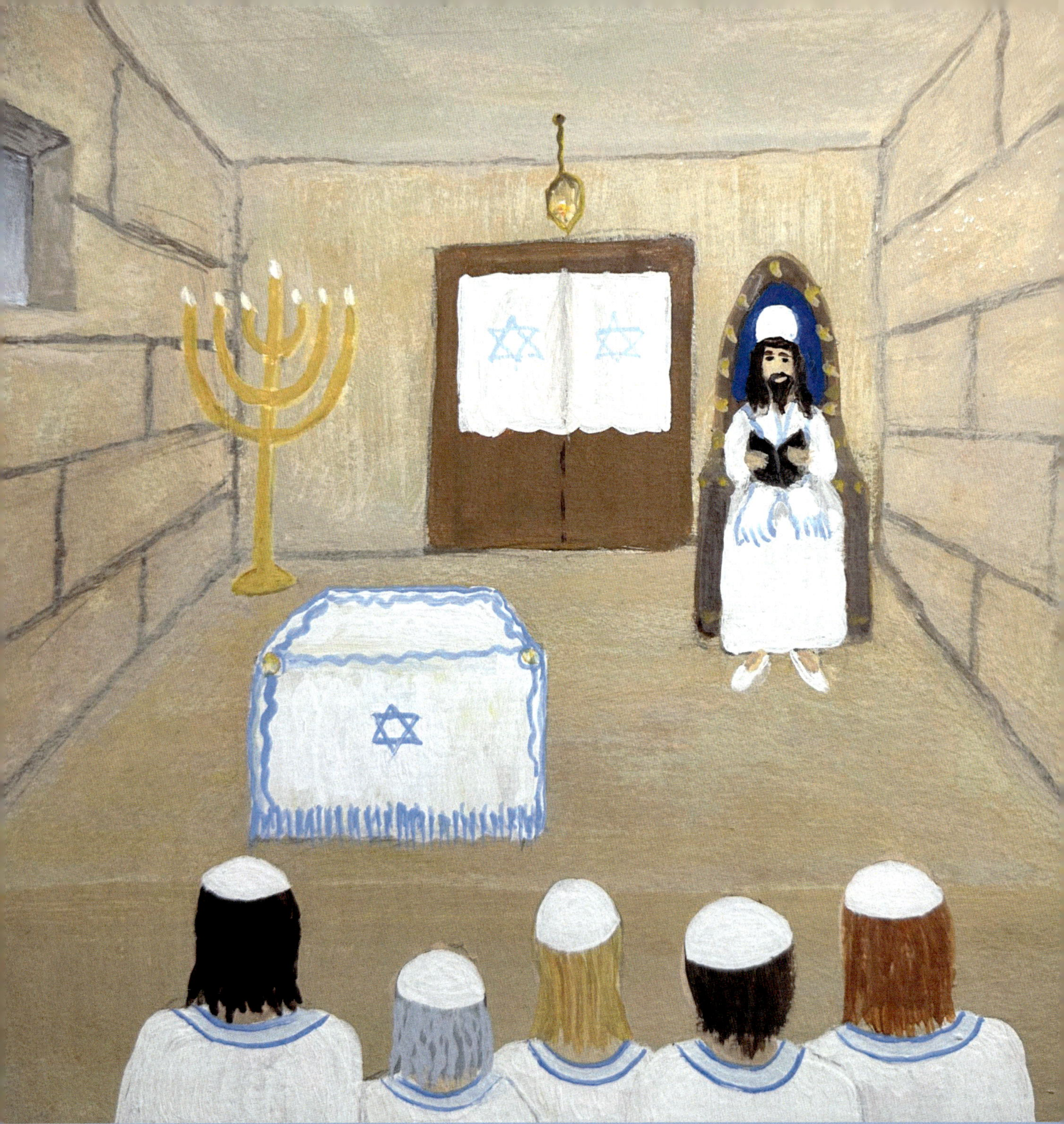

Once there was a farmer whose custom it was to spend all day praying on Yom Kippur. The synagogue was led by the famous Rabbi Yehuda, known for his kindness and ability to deliver a great sermon.

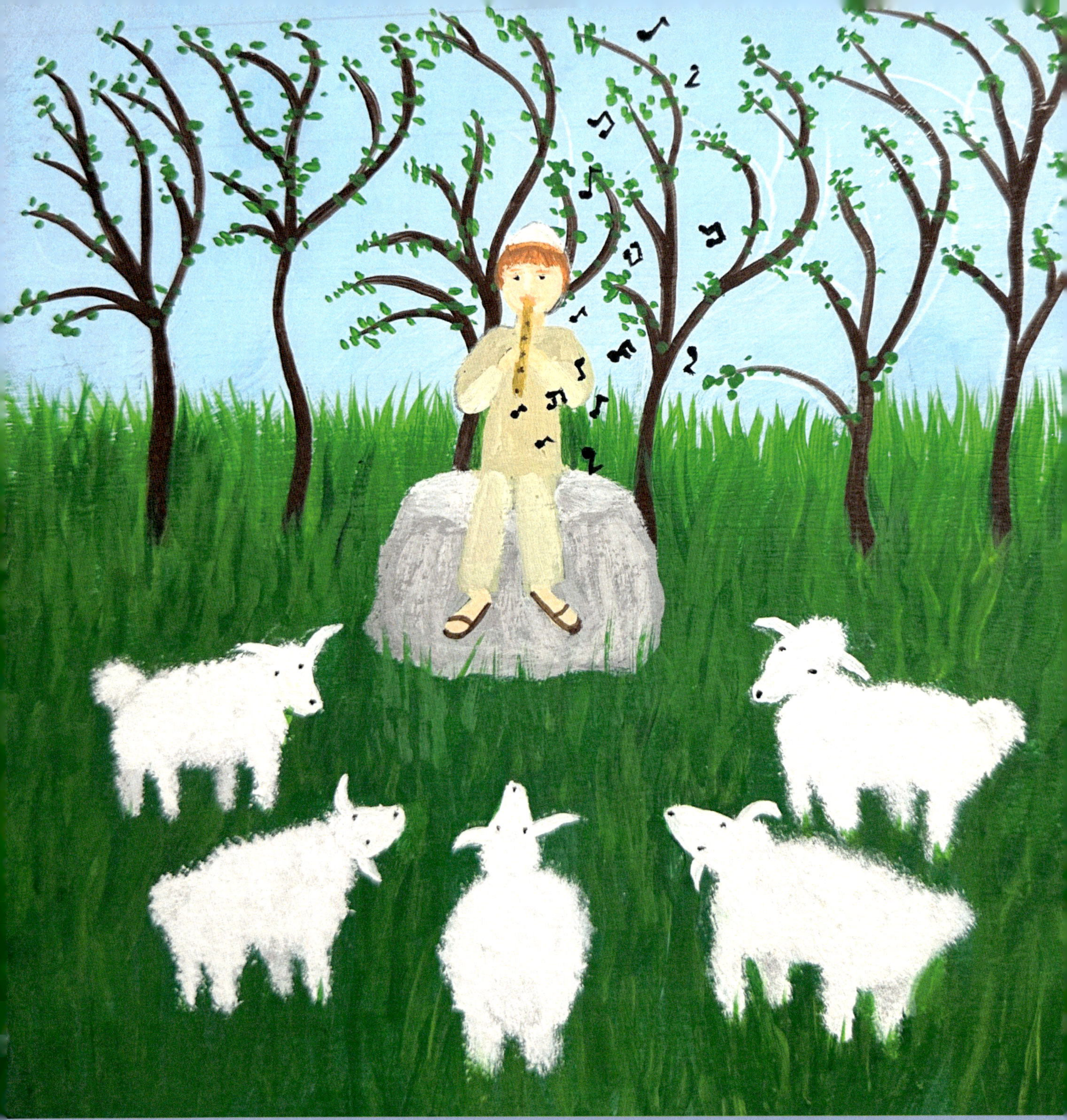

Because his son Meir did not know how to pray in Hebrew, the farmer left him at home to tend to the sheep. With his reed pipe, the boy played beautiful, joyful melodies, and the sheep in the pasture would follow him wherever he went. Never did the boy ever allow a single sheep to get lost.

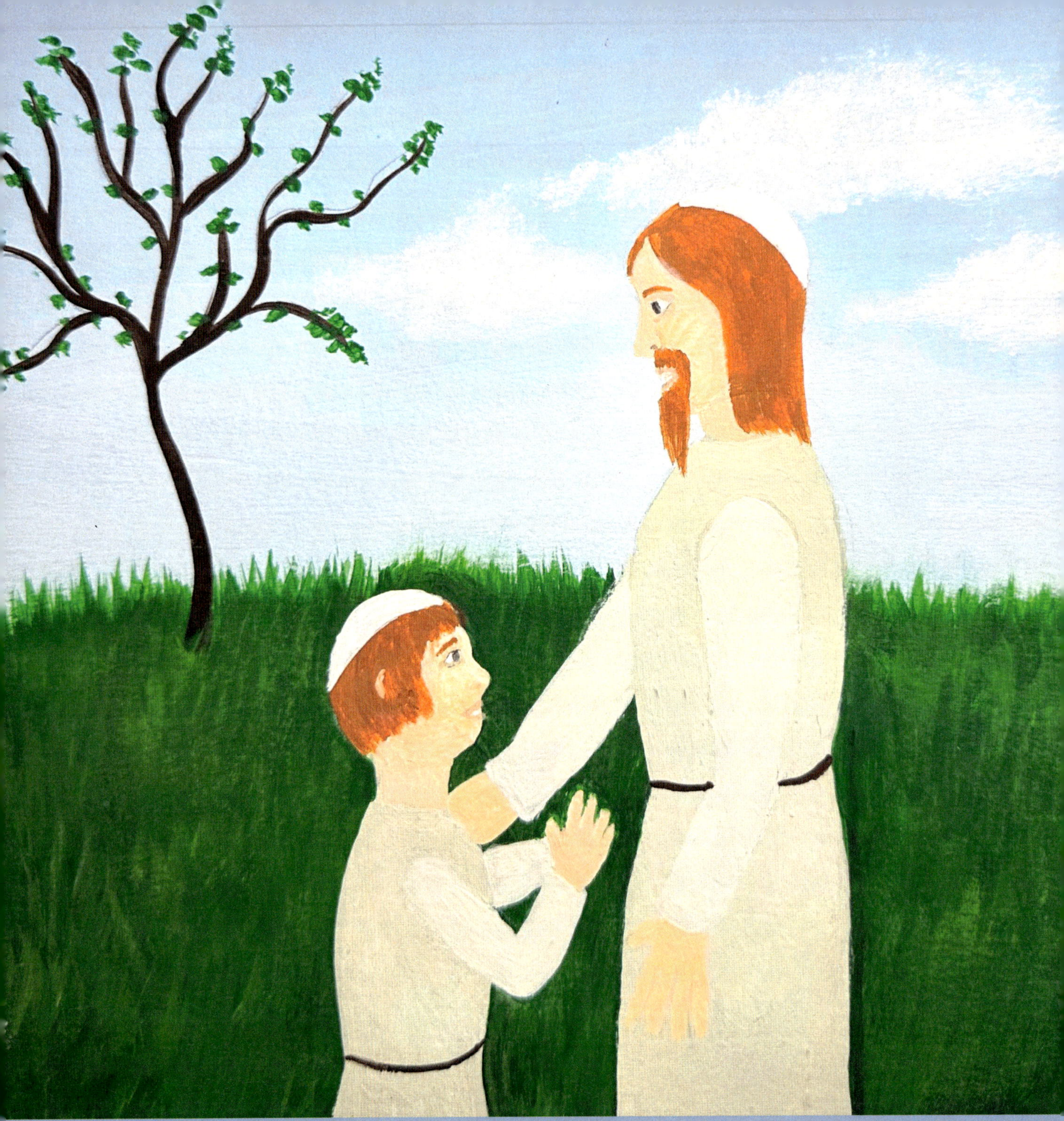

Each year before Yom Kippur Meir would ask his father whether he could come to with him to synagogue and pray. And each year he got the same answer: "Stay home and play your songs for the sheep."

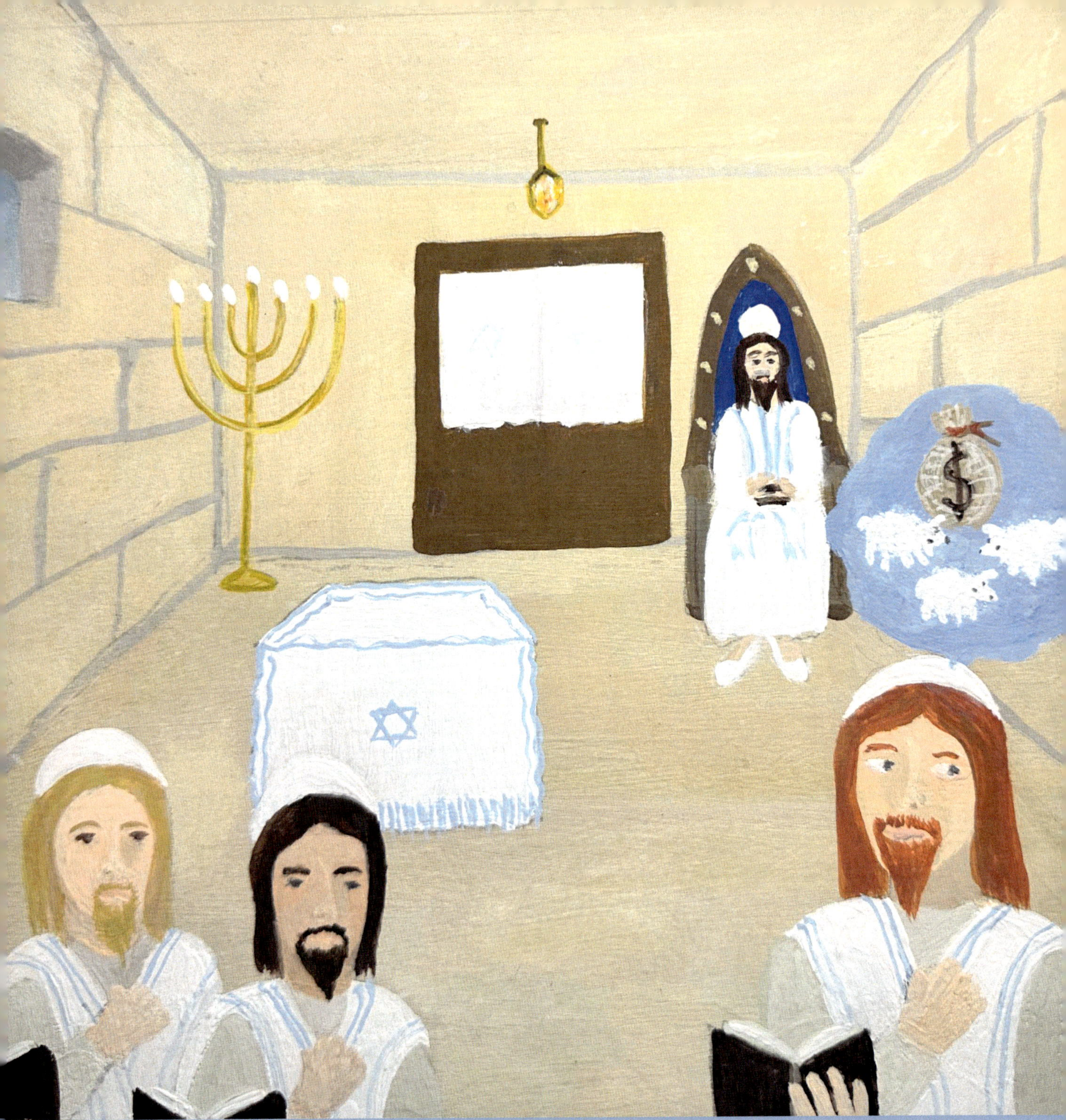

This year's Yom Kippur was incredibly special for the farmer. Rabbi Yehuda asked him to take a seat of honor by the eastern wall where the more learned people always sat. The farmer opened his prayer book, and his lips formed the words of the prayers. And as everyone else beat their breasts with their fists while confessing their prayers, the farmer's mind was not on the words he was saying. He was thinking other things. "If I can buy a hundred bushels of corn next week, I could sell them and make a lot of money. I wonder what the cost will be of a hundred bushels?"

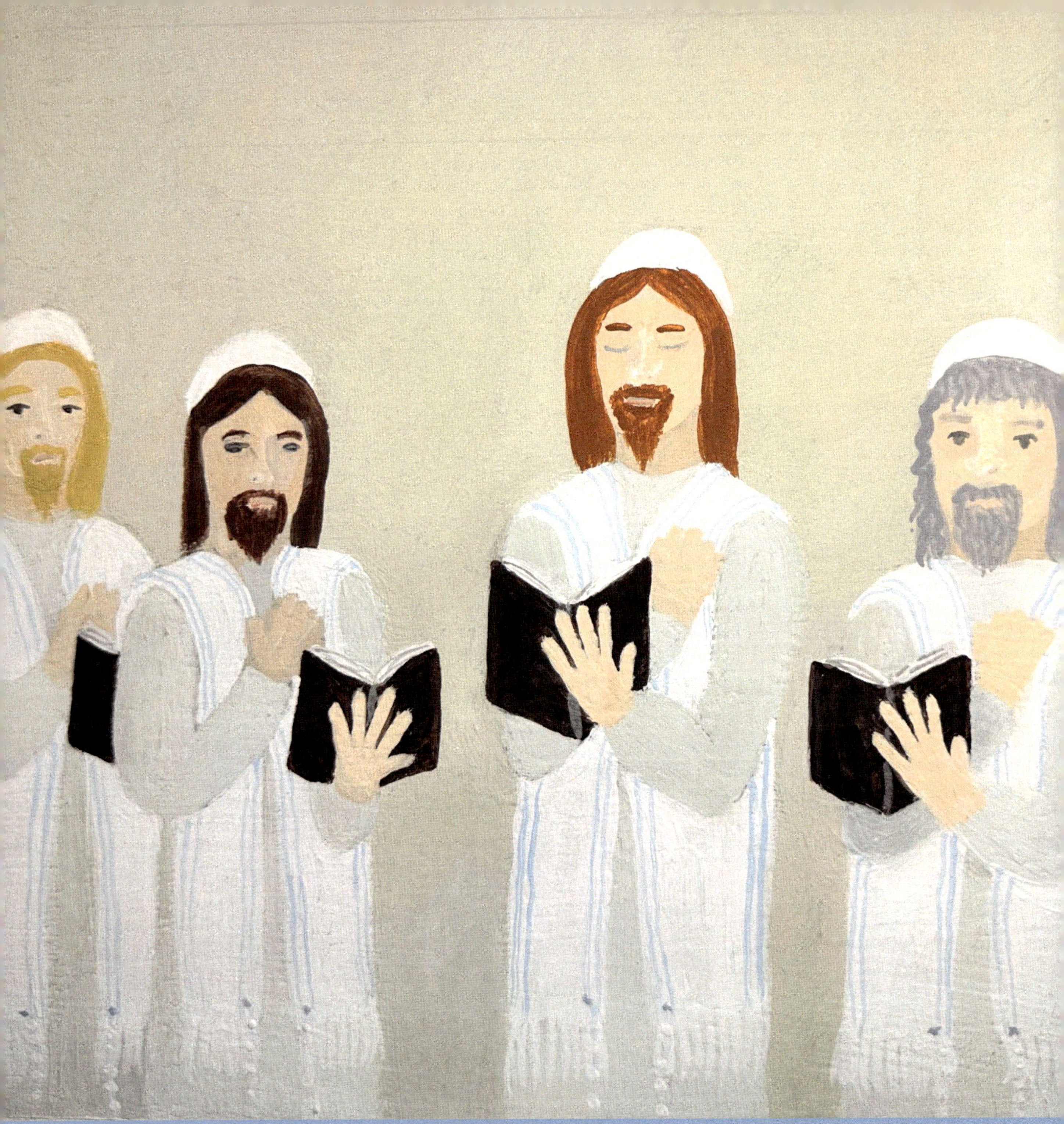

As his fist beat against his chest again, the farmer closed his eyes and thought about how wonderful it will be at the end of the day when he can break his fast and finally eat.

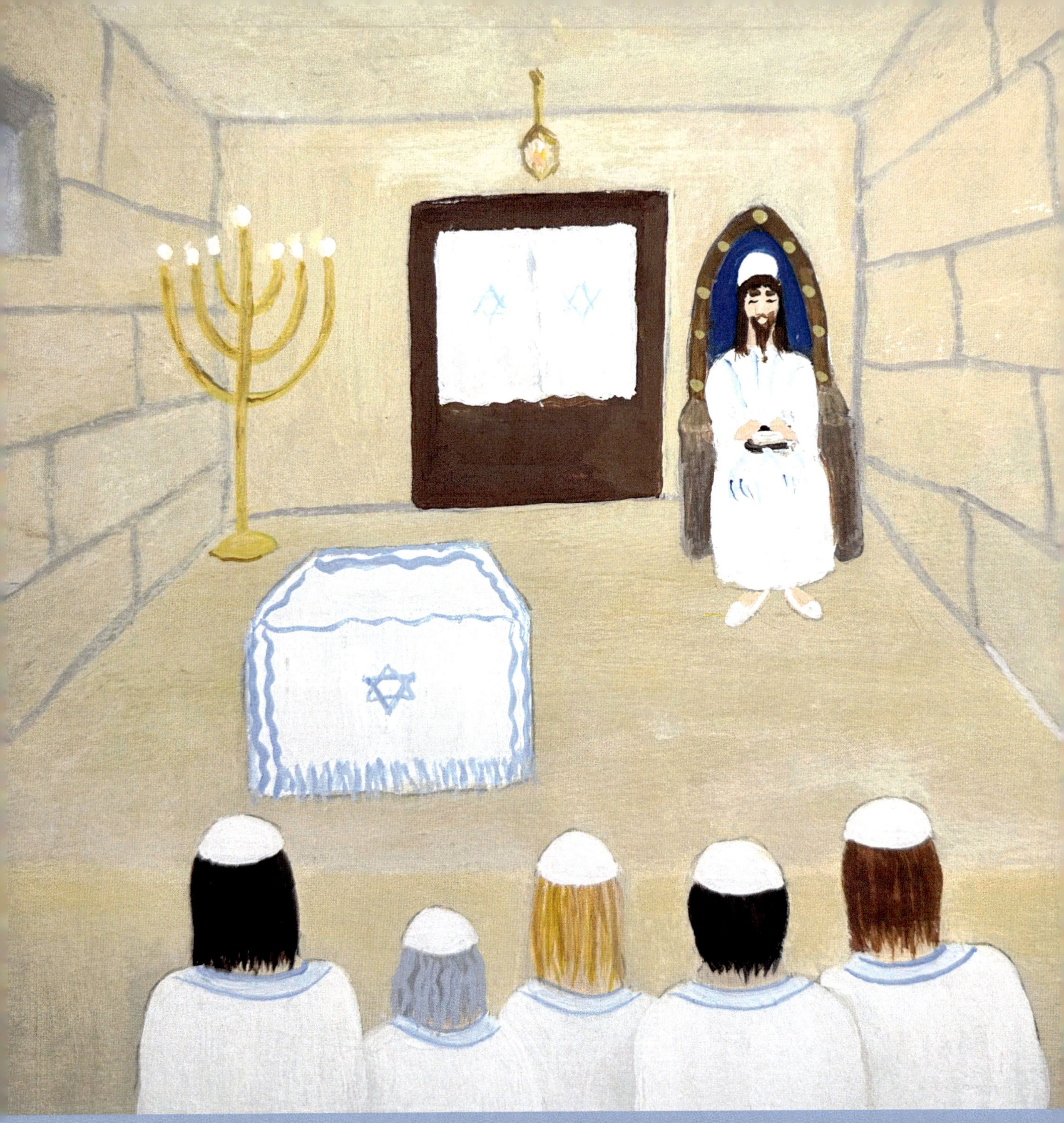

Hours passed and the sun had sunk in the west. It was getting darker by the minute. It was time to begin the last part of the service. But for some reason Rabbi Yehuda was not starting the Neila service. He didn't ask God to shut the gates of heaven and seal the congregants in the Book of Life. Instead, he chanted hymn after hymn and begged God to listen to all of the prayers of all the people.

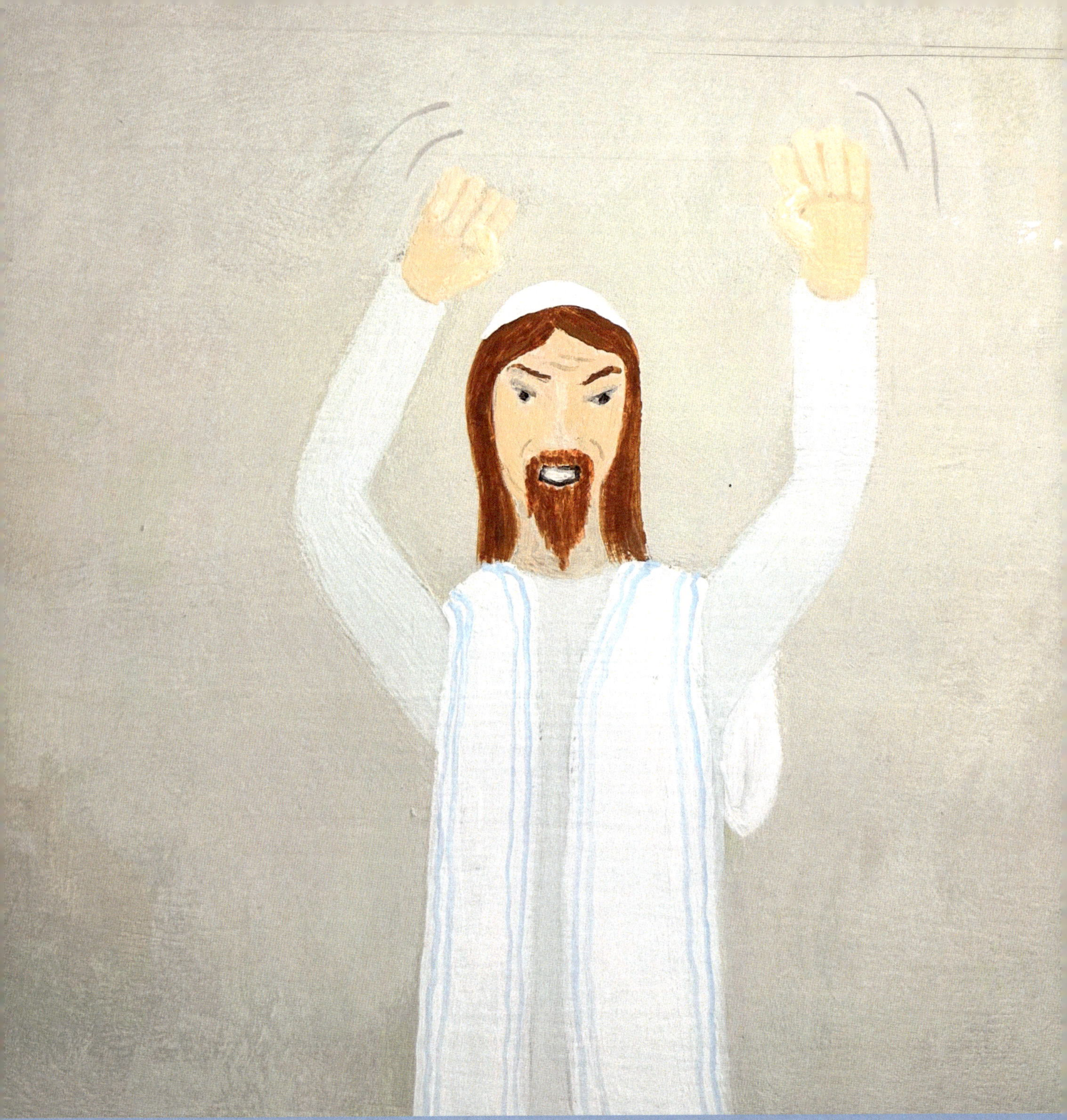

The farmer began to get angry, as did many in the congregation.

What is Rabbi Yehuda doing? Why isn't he finishing the

service.? Everyone is hungry.

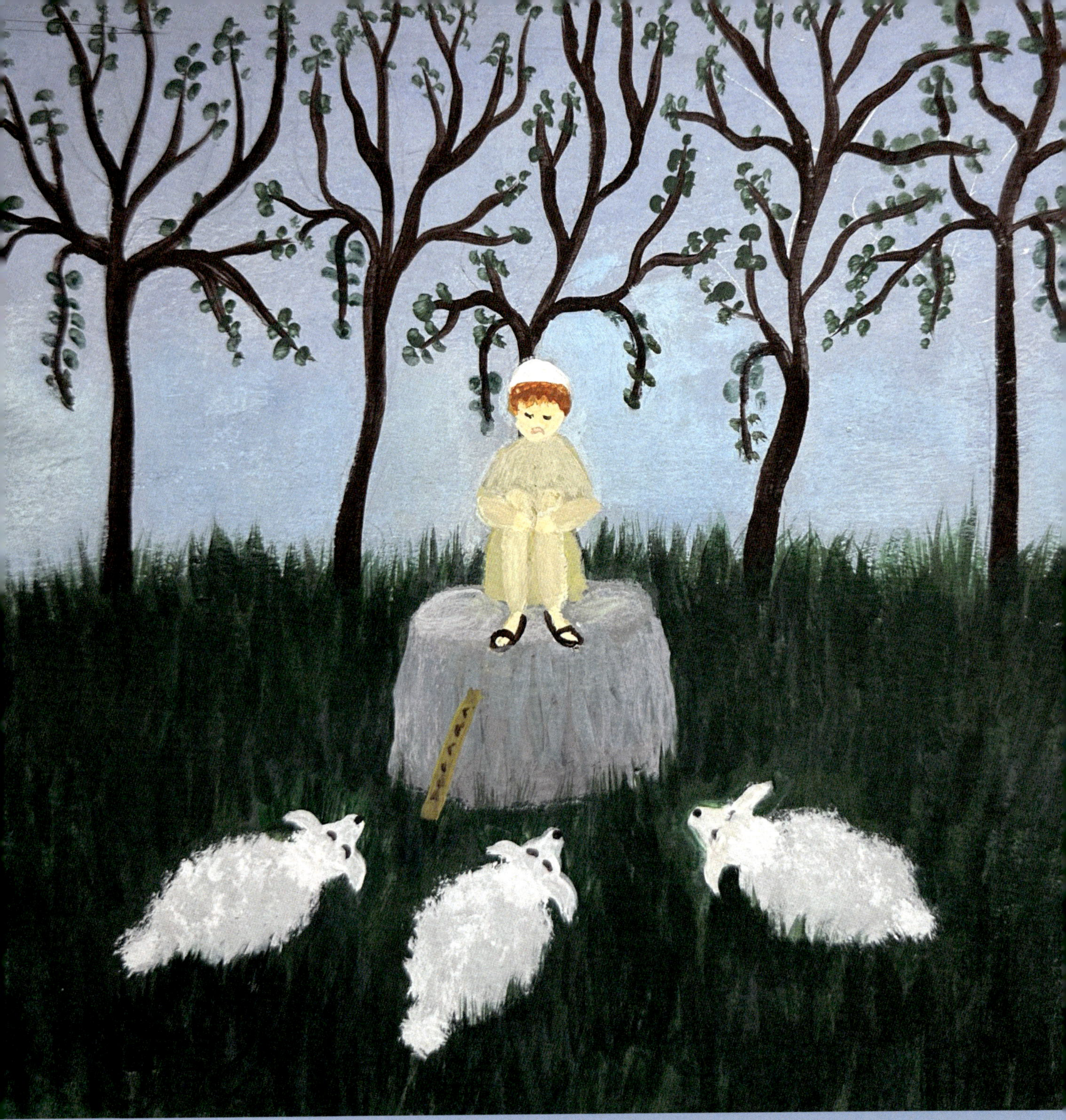

Back at the pasture the day was exceptionally long as well for little Meir. The sheep had eaten their fill of grass and not one had been lost. But it was a very hot day. Meir was getting very thirsty, and hungry too.

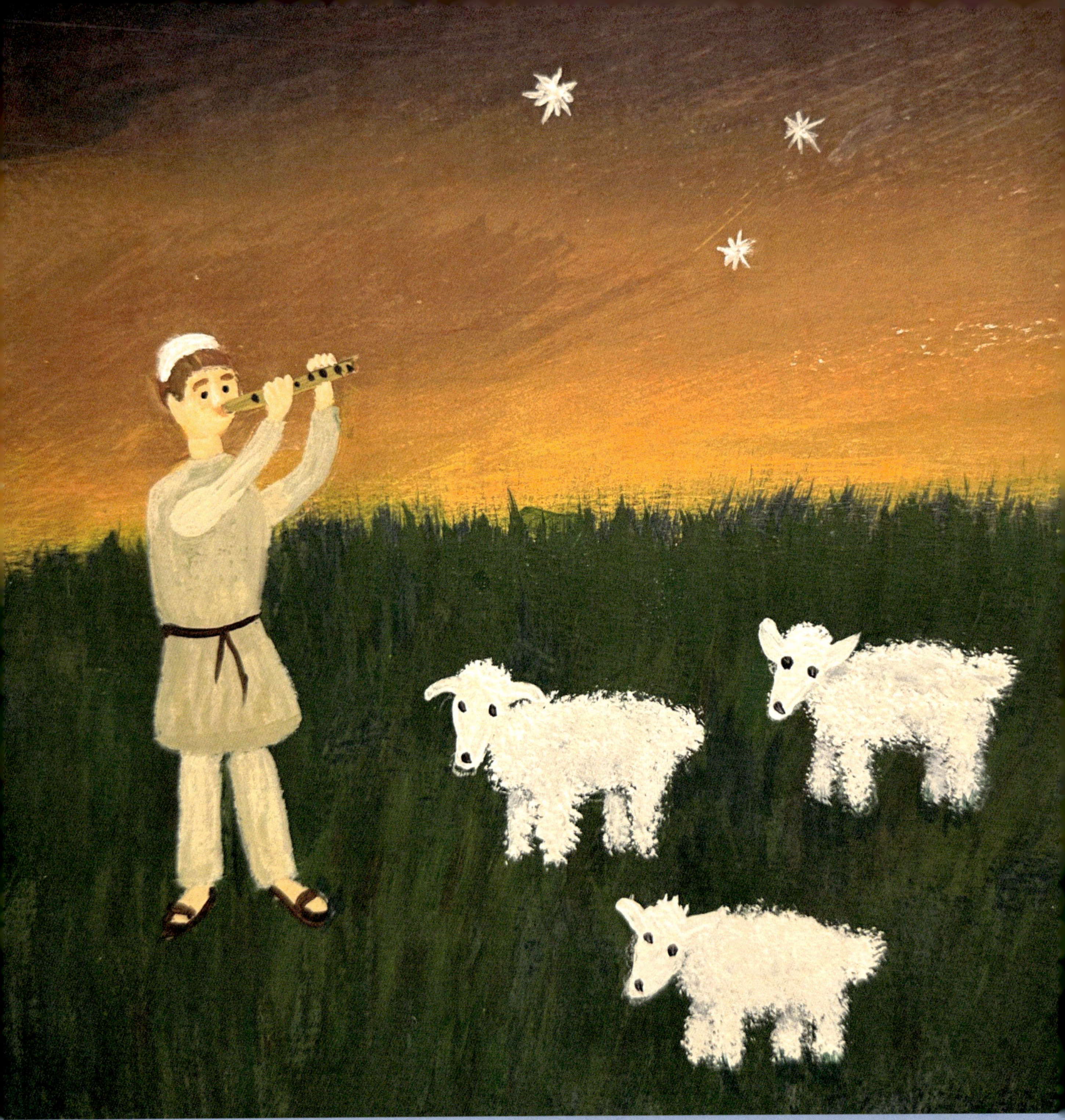

As the sun sank, Meir picked up his reed pipe. This time, before playing, he looked to the three stars in the sky and said: "Dear God, I do not know any of the prayers. But I can play the pipe, so what I will do for You now is to play You this tune that I wrote just for You."

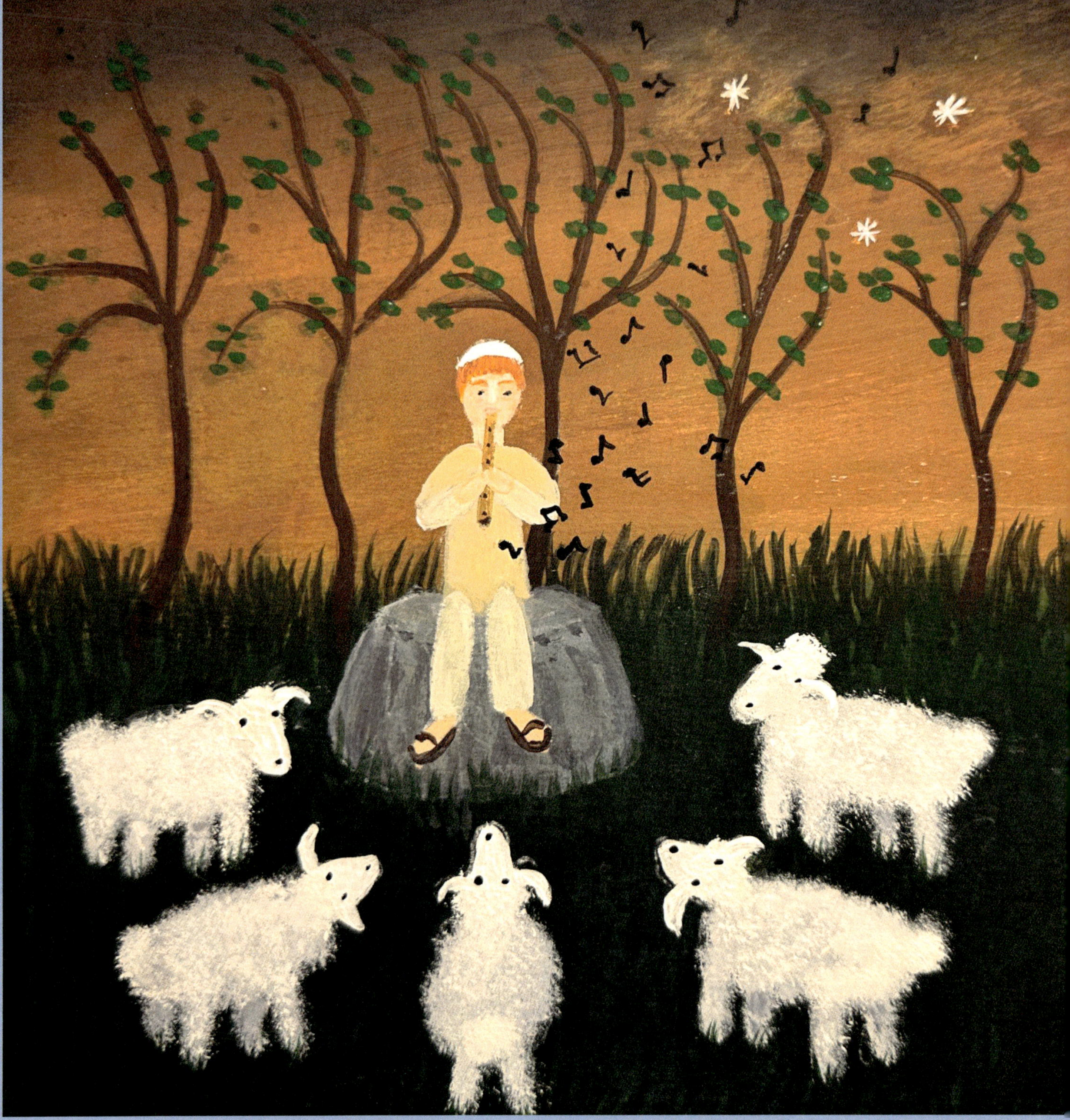

On his pipe, Meir began to play a beautiful, soft and tranquil melody that he made up all by himself. As he played it, the tall grass all around began to wave back and forth, and the trees seemed to sway in the breeze. The boy's heart, mind and soul were in the special tune that he played for God as the stars twinkled.

תקיעה גדולה

At that exact moment, Rabbi Yehuda began chanting the prayers of the Neila service. "Our Father and King, accept our prayer. Our Father our God, seal us in Your Book of Life." And then he picked up the *shofar*, the ram's horn, and blew a long blast that bellowed in every corner of the room. Yom Kippur had ended.

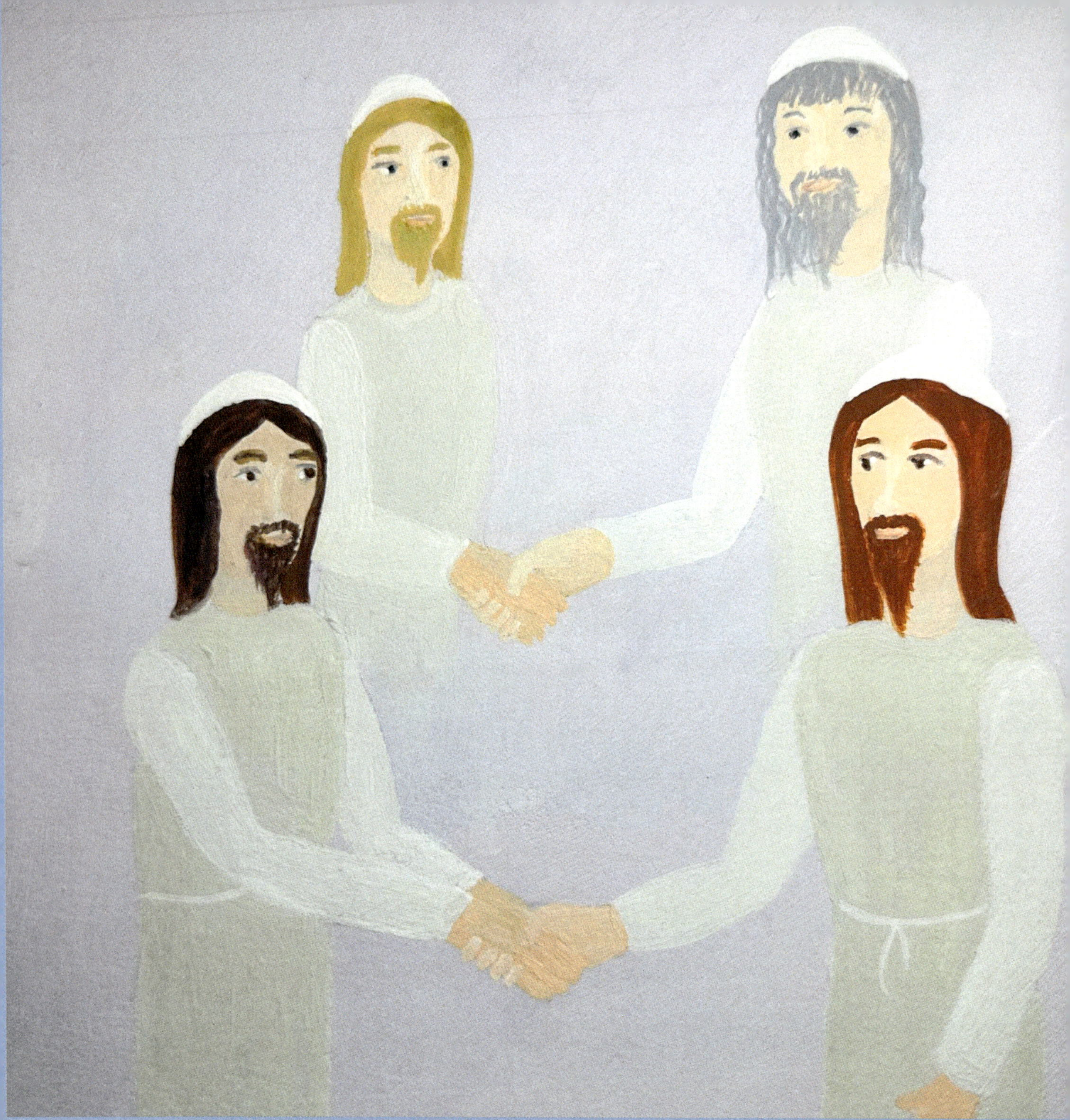

Each member wished the other *L'shana tova*—a happy New Year. Then the farmer could not resist and approached Rabbi Yehuda. "*Shana tova*," he said.

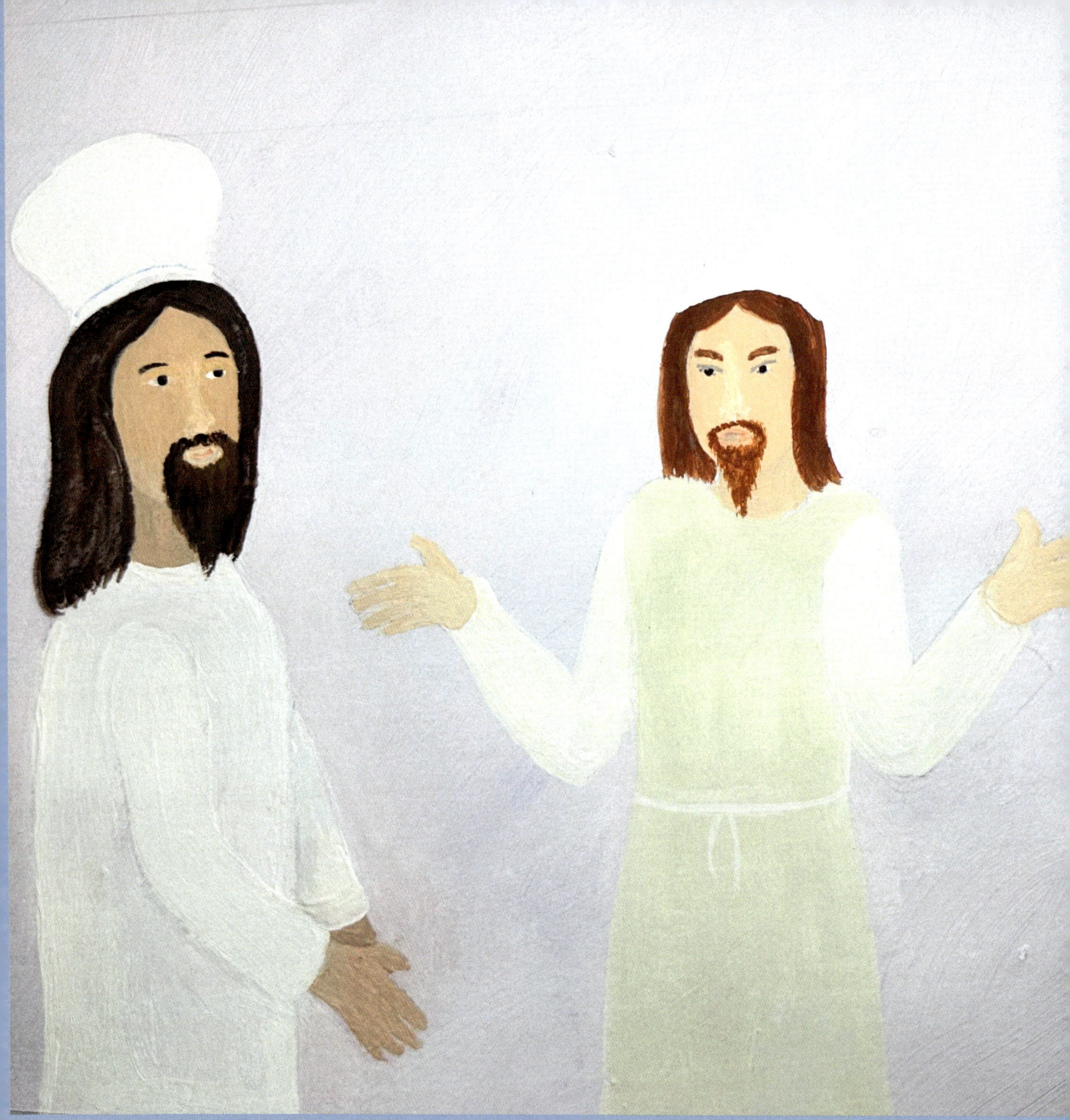

"I have a question for you that I am sure everyone in the congregation is also asking. "Why did you wait so long to begin the Neila service? Why did you wait so long to end Yom Kippur?"

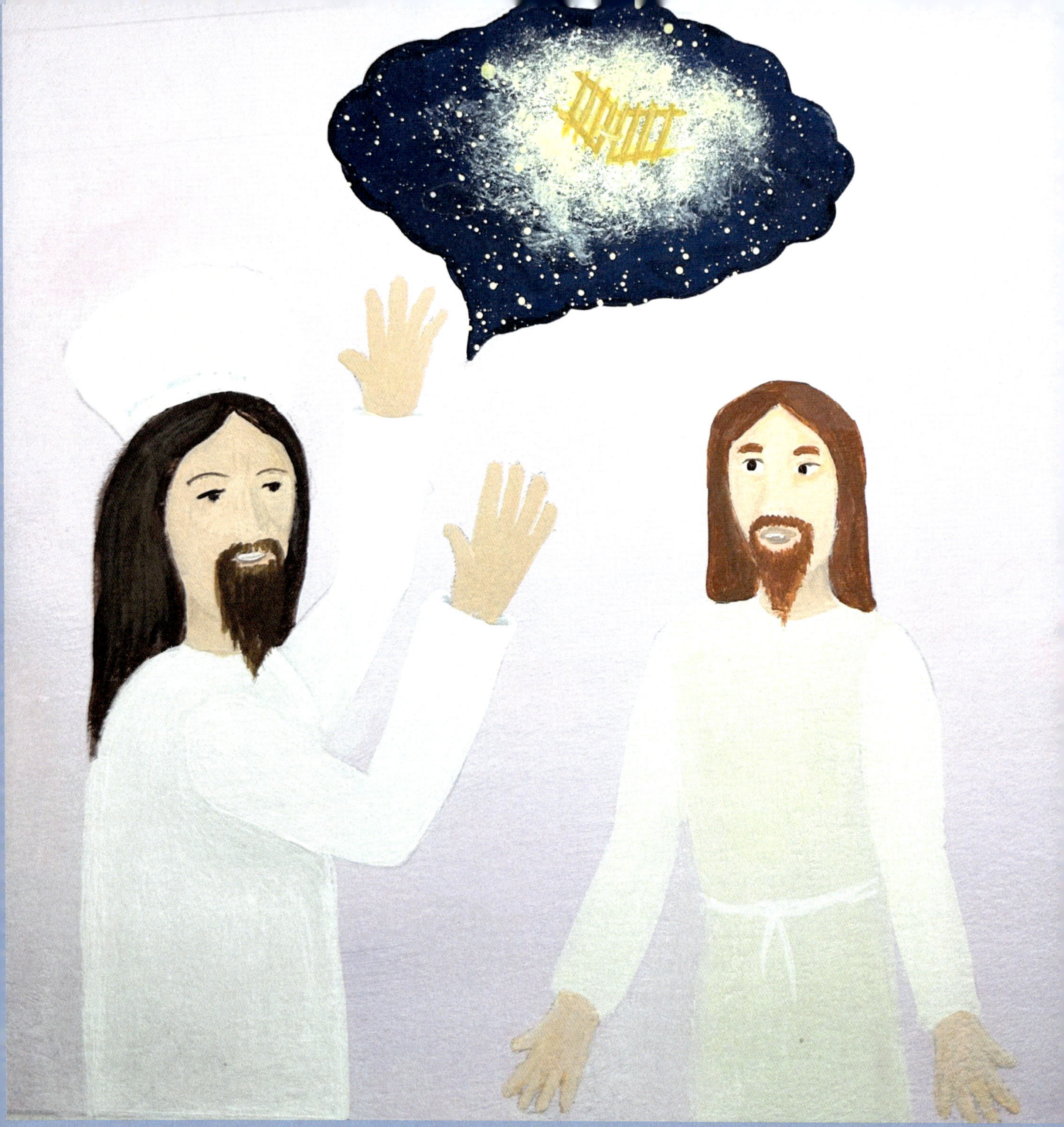

Rabbi Yehuda looked straight into the farmer's eyes. "I had a vision," he said. In my vision I saw that the gates of heaven were closed, and our prayers were not at all reaching God."

"Why?" asked the farmer.

The Rabbi answered: "I think because the prayers of the congregation did not come from their heart and soul. And how could I end services knowing that God was not really listening to our prayers, because our minds were elsewhere?"

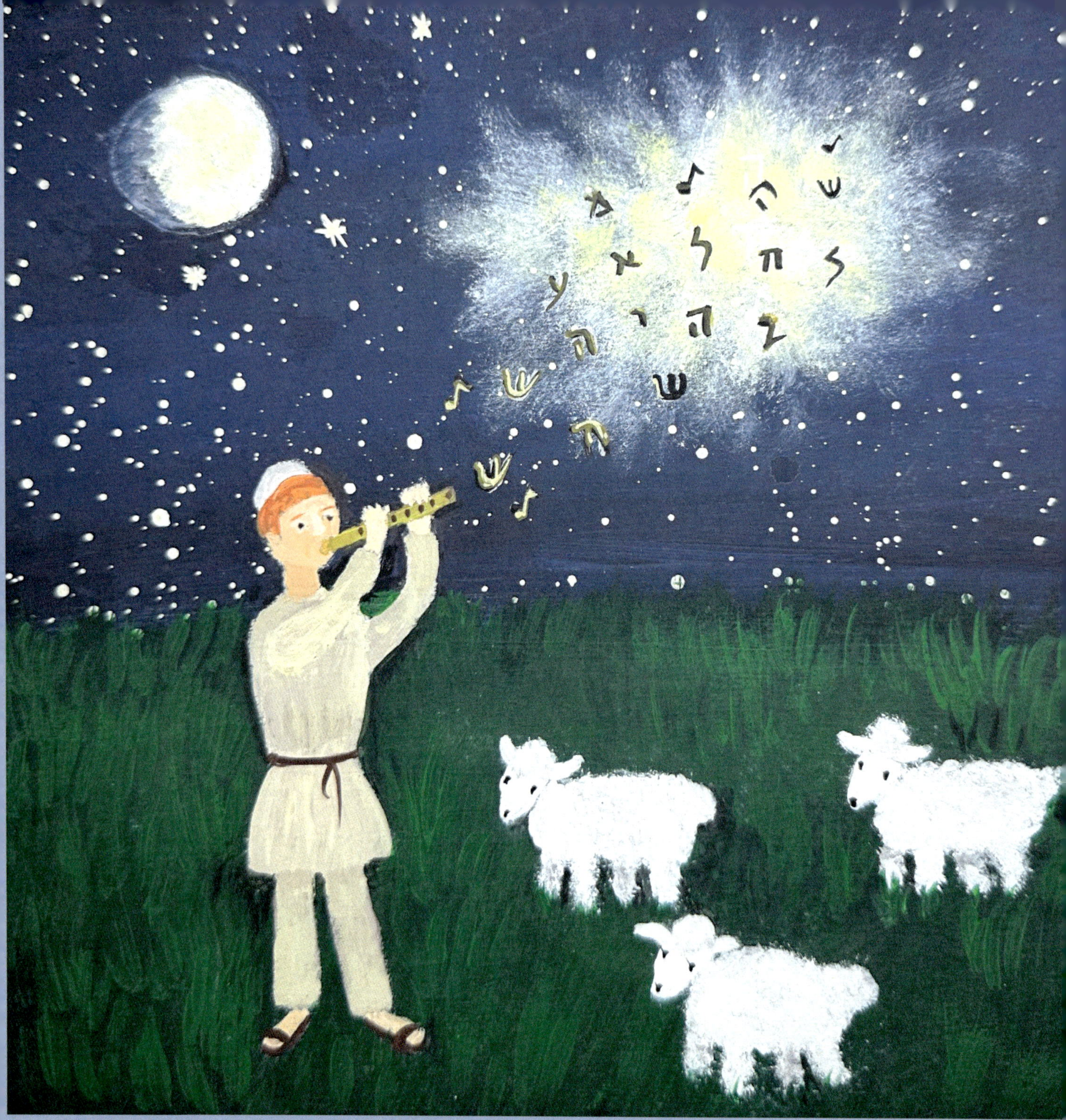

"But in another vision, I heard a beautiful melody played on a reed people and saw the gates of heaven open up. And our prayers went up to God because God had to open the gates so that the melody could enter."

"But why?" asked the farmer. "It was just a melody played on a flute."

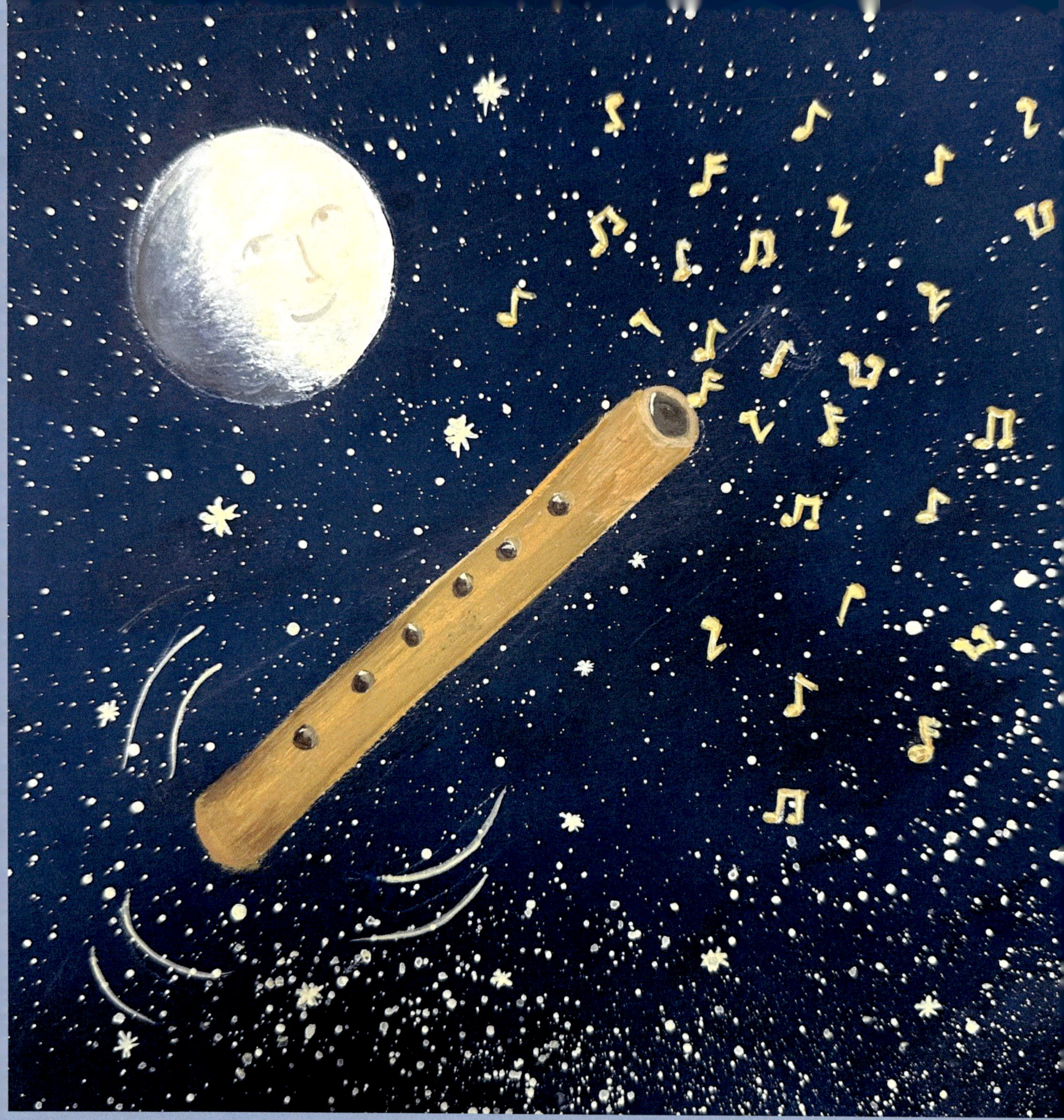

"Because" said the rabbi, "whoever played that melody to God played it with all his heart and soul. It was true prayer. It was true service of the heart."

The End

Glossary

Neila: Hebrew word meaning "to close", it signifies the concluding service on *Yom Kippur*, the Jewish fast day of atonement.

Yom Kippur: Jewish Day of Atonement, generally regarded as the holiest day of the year. It is marked by fasting and offering prayers for Divine forgiveness.

**Other Titles Available from
Higher Ground Books & Media:**

Here Come the Seagulls by Ron Isaacs
Look to the Birds by Ron Isaacs
Midnight the Holy Cow by Ron Isaacs
The Sheep With the Golden Horns by Ron Isaacs
Song Heard Round the World by Ron Isaacs
Sing to God: Halleluyah! By Ron Isaacs
Moses and the Extra Ten by Ron Isaacs
Prayer for the World: Song of the Grass by Ron Isaacs
Reba Loves Shabbat by Ron Isaacs
I Am Hanukkah by Ron Isaacs
I Am Passover by Ron Isaacs
I Am Purim by Ron Isaacs

Rudy the Maintenance Man by Kerry Olitzky
Sam & Sophie by Kerry Olitzky

Grumble D. Grumble Learns to Smile by Rebecca Benston
On a Hike with Pixie Trist and Bo by Charlotte Hopkins

Add these titles to your collection today!
www.highergroundbooksandmedia.com

HIGHER GROUND BOOKS & MEDIA
AN INDEPENDENT PUBLISHER

Do you have a story to tell?

Higher Ground Books & Media is an independent Christian-based publisher specializing in stories of triumph! Our purpose is to empower, inspire, and educate through the sharing of personal experiences. We are always looking for great, new stories to add to our collection. If you're looking for a publisher, get in touch with us today!

Please be sure to visit our website for our submission guidelines.

http://www.highergroundbooksandmedia.com/submission-guidelines

HGBM SERVICES

Help For Authors!

HGBM Services offers a variety of writing and coaching services for aspiring authors! We can help with editing, manuscript critiques, self-publishing, and much more! Get in touch today to see how we can help you make your dream of becoming an author a reality!

*****

We also offer social media marketing services for authors, small businesses, and non-profit organizations. Let us help you get the word out about your book, your projects, and your mission. We offer great rates, quality promos, consistent communication, and a personal touch!

http://www.highergroundbooksandmedia.com/editing-writing-services

Need Bulk Copies?

If you would like to order bulk copies of this book or any other title at Higher Ground Books & Media, please contact us at highergroundbooksandmedia@gmail.com.

We offer discounts for purchases of 20 or more copies. Excellent for small groups, book clubs, classrooms, etc.

Get in touch today and get a set of great stories for your students or group members.

Made in the USA
Middletown, DE
15 October 2024